CONCISE PUN-ISHING DICTIONARY

for English Speakers

Foreword by Professor David Crystal

IP 00/2013/4336, registered 22/08/2013
ISBN-978-84-617-1742-2

To my wife, Carmen Rosa

ACKNOWLEDGEMENTS

I would like to express my thanks to Professor David Crystal who said that the dictionary I was then beginning to compile would "interest English speakers, not just the native ones"; to "agentleman" Guy Rose, fiction writers Rachel Abbot and Talli Roland and to my long-time dear friend Mary Willix, for their inestimable words of encouragement; to my colleague at the University of La Laguna, Clive Tyrell, who proofread the manuscript and made useful suggestions to improve the text, and last, but not least, to Ana Eva Felipe, the illustrator, for her beautiful drawings.

FOREWORD

Puns are catching. It only takes one person in a conversation to make a pun and others try to outpun them. Children take to puns at an early age in their language play. And we admire really ingenious instances - as shown by the mock-groan-decibel (MGD) level they readily elicit.

Punning has been part of English since Anglo-Saxon times, especially fostered - as Pablo Dominguez suggests in his Introduction - by its many monosyllabic homophones. The practice is probably as old as human language itself. 'In the beginning', as Samuel Beckett says in *Murphy*, 'was the pun'.

This book takes MGD levels to previously unattained heights. I've never seen a collection as linguistically imaginative and entertaining as this one. The ***Concise Pun-ishing Dictionary*** is an absolute delight.

David Crystal, Holyhead, UK, April 2014

INTRODUCTORY NOTE

> "Then, Hermogenes, the giving of names can hardly be, as you imagine, a trifling matter or a task for trifling or casual persons"
>
> (Socrates in Plato's *Cratylus*)

To: undisclosed recipients

Considering that there have been excellent English dictionaries available ever since Nathaniel Bailey published his ***Universal Etymological English Dictionary*** in 1721, you may wonder why somebody who is not a native speaker of English dared to write a dictionary for speakers of a language that is not his own. Well, the reason is obvious; no other similar dictionary exists that I know of which offers the same characteristics as mine. ***Concise Pun-nishing dictionary*** is not only totally different from others in content, such as Richard Hall's ***Sniglets*** (1984), Joan Cooke's in The Oxford English Fictionary http://oefictionary.tumblr.com/or ***The Meaning of Liff*** (1983), but also regarding the approach.

It is a well-known fact that the use of puns and word play serve the purpose of giving pleasure and, at the same time, adding punch to what is being said. Instances of this particular use can be found in all languages, but it is, no doubt, the existence of a great number of homophones in English that makes it a well-suited tongue for this kind of verbal exercise.

There are additional types of word-play which are not only amusing but may also be appropriately used in certain circumstances. If you leaf through the pages of this dictionary, you will see that all the entries are built upon a particularly subjective view of familiar words which, by altering their spelling slightly, acquire a new shade of meaning, though still being pronounced the same or practically the same. And, of course, these 'new' words can be very convenient to refer to specific actions, personal circumstances, etc. Thus, **"abwhore"** is to detest a certain kind of women for moral reasons; **"abdoctor"** is a medical person who was found guilty of kidnapping patients; **"binister"** is a person who becomes head of a government department for the second time; **"copiss"** is a group of bushes and undergrowth at the side of a road where drivers often stop to "water the flowers"; **"floot"** is a stolen wind instrument; **"Evesdrop"** is what Adam's wife could never do; **"gosship"** is tittle-tattle about other people's private lives while on a cruise; **"impertenant"** is an insolent lodger; **"pshychologist"** is a therapist specialized in treating people who suffer from timidity; **"whatshit"**, a vulgar manner of referring to the name of something that we forget, etc.

If, after reading the samples above, you are still unsure whether you would like to buy the book, I recommend that you see a specialist in, for example, eating disorders; something must be wrong with your sense of humour !

Pablo Domínguez

"A word is dead when it's been said, some say. I say it just begins to live that day." *Emily Dickinson*

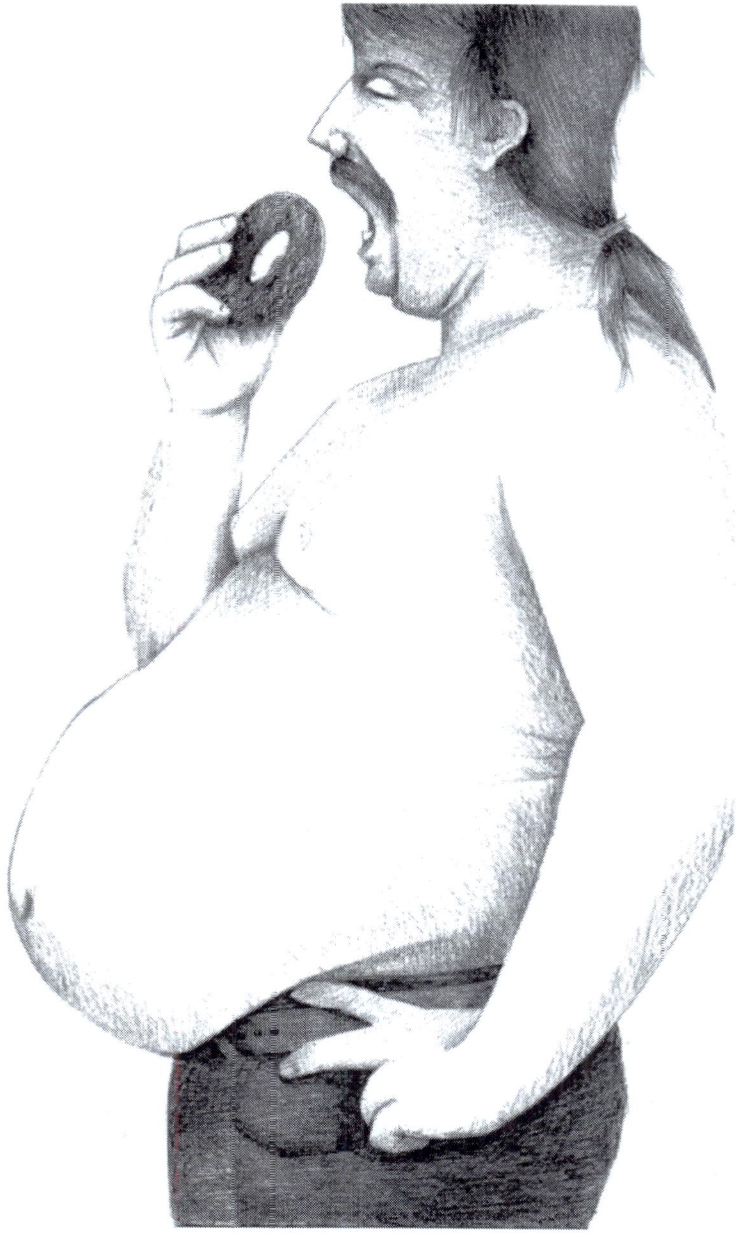

Abdominable

Abanden: leave a hidden hangout of thieves

Abbraviation: shortened versions of aircraft

Abdoctor: medical person who was found guilty of kidnapping patients

Abdominable: unpleasantly obese

Aberryation: unexpected change in the taste of simple fruits (blackberries, strawberries, or blueberries) in which the seeds are embedded

Abillety: skill to billet armed forces in proper premises

Abluetions: the act of washing oneself with indigo coloured water

Abnormale: freakish male creature

Aboartion: the act of giving birth before the pig has been properly developed

Abombinate: bombard a population with utter hate

Abroach: come close to a lady in order to snatch the jewel she is wearing on her blouse or coat

Abscent: pleasant smell which is not there any more

Abcsex: swelling, usually painful, in the pubic area of a person

Absentea: infusion which has been drunk up

Abstruce: agreement between enemies to stop fighting which is too difficult to believe

Abwhore: detest a certain kind of women for moral reasons

Abyde: live near

Acclamotion: meeting proposal passed unanimously

Accommadate: fix a particular period of time for updating the use of the punctuation mark (,) in English

Accomodating: the act of putting up two people who are having a romantic relationship

Accomplease: person who is happy to help another to commit a crime

Accredictation: official recognition of an institution or of certain public figures like lawyers, diplomats, etc., which is read out for another person to transcribe it

Accreation: longer than expected duration that it takes an artist to finish their work

Acher: person who feels a strong pain after measuring an area of land of 4840 square yards

Achecidental: of a painful injury caused by chance to a patient in the dental surgery / office

Achoir: obtain something by singing in a group

Acknee: inflammatory disease of the skin on the middle joint of the leg

Acolight: person carrying a torch or lamp who helps a priest to perform a religious service when there is a power cut

Acoredance: the main part of choreography agreed to be reserved for the prima ballerina

Acquiessence: agreement on only the basics of a situation

Acrew: employ more people to work on a ship or plane

Acravat: circus entertainer who performs difficult feats wearing a scarf round the neck

Accrademic: professor at the University of Ghana

Acropolice: body of people employed to keep order at the Parthenon in Athens

Acsession: meeting during which somebody takes up a position

Addverse: unfavourable poetic advertisement

Addvertiser: person who writes poetic adds

Addvice: contribute to commit illegal acts following somebody's recommendation

Addvisable: recommended advertisement

Adequote: acceptable citation

Admirall: senior naval officer who really likes everything related to the navy

Administraitor: person who manages the affairs of an organization but is disloyal to its members

Admissable: that may be allowed in spite of having failed to attend something

Admoneysh: advice against wasting one's monthly payments

Admunition: warning informing the Army of the need to supply more bullets, bombs, etc.

Adoor: love at the entrance of a building

Adoorable: very nice door

Adulltery: unexciting extramarital sexual relations

Adverteasement: notice of some kind intended to poke fun at somebody or something

Advintage: something favourable to a specific purpose which in past times was considered of a high quality

Affidavid: written oath in which people called David promise to tell the truth

Afictionado: fan of reading novels

Afrikaants: South African branch of philosophical thought in the tradition of the *Critique of Pure Reason*

Aftermass: feeling of relief for having fulfilled one's religious obligations

Aftermoon: lunar time from 24:00 PM until about 06:00AM

Agender: list of things to be done which varies according to the sex of the person

Agentleman: honest, respectful person who acts on behalf of another

Aggloberation: jumbled number of balloons as those seen in Cappadocia skies

Aggluttonation: the practice of eating to excess different foods mixed together

Aggrandice. large piece of frozen water

Agonice: suffer great pain caused by extremely low temperatures

Agrophobia: fear of living in rural areas

Ahmen!: common exclamation made by women to show exasperation about their husbands /male partners

Airadicate: uproot something violently as when a gale-force wind blows

Airate: the cost of oxygenating something

Airfair: a reasonable price for a plane ticket

Akingbow: standing position adopted by some medieval monarchs after using a large weapon for shooting arrows

Alibye: defendant's painful exclamation after the judge demolished his arguments pleading not guilty

Alimoney: allowance that a court orders to pay to the wife or husband after a legal separation or divorce

Allowonce: lump sum of money granted one time only

Alphabetter: unsuccessful attempts by some proponents of an English spelling reform to change the letters of this language

Alreadish: cooked food that can be served straight away

Altaration: change in the holy platform of a church where mass is celebrated

Amaizement: overwhelming surprise to see the devastating damages to the crop of corn caused by a violent storm

Amatorish: of a lover who lacks professional skill

Ambushador: US diplomatic representative during the Bush mandates

Amewsment park: cats' funfair

Amiaowbility: attribute of cats who are pleasant and friendly

Akingbow

Ancillorry: large auxiliary vehicle

Animossyty: an old fashioned way of showing hate

Annacquainted: unfamiliar with Ann

Antarktic: large boat known to exist before Noah's time, traces of which have been found in the most southern part of the Earth

Antenner: inexpensive aerial

Anthrasite: piece of ground where a certain type of coal can be found

Antiaquarium: building in which rare and surviving prehistoric fish are kept

Aparthide: in South Africa, segregation of non-white people who were later concealed from sight

Aperil: a month traditionally known for its dangerous natural events

Applicaution: formal request done with wily tactfulness

Apocalips: disastrous damage caused by the sun to somebody's lips

Apologee: something said emphatically to show that one is sorry for something done

Apostrophy: written mark on a winning prize to emphasize its value

Appetight: strong desire to eat which is self-controlled in order not to show eagerness

Appiecement: the act of dividing something into fair quantities which satisfy everybody

Appreysal: careful evaluation of an animal that has been hunted

Approprettily: of something pilfered in a delicate way

Aquidistant: at the same distance from a river, lake or sea

Aqueuemulate: line up things collected over a period of time

Aridzona: name sometimes used to refer to very dry dessert like the Mojave dessert in North America

Arkane: mysterious boat built by Noah for sheltering his family and all kind of animals

Armshouse: place for the reception of weapons to support and aid the rebels in a war

Armystease: mock agreement between countries to stop a war temporarily which irritates those who take part in the fighting

Aromantic: pleasant fragrance arising from someone who is sentimental

Arreign: criticize severely a king for, for example, shooting elephants while on a safari in Africa

Arsannals:	record of weapons stored every year in a government building
Artickle:	amusing piece of writing in a newspaper or magazine
Artison:	skilled workman's male child
Artory:	blood vessel of a member of the British Conservative Party
Aspectre:	frightening appearance of something/one
Aspersians:	derogatory remarks about Iranians
Assascene:	situation in which a murder takes place
Assalt:	attacking some by throwing salt at them
Assaylant:	person who mentions what he/she is about to do before attacking somebody else
Assiduos:	related to two pairs of entertainers who come to a certain place regularly to give performances
Assixstance:	help given to a person for the sixth time
Astronought:	zero space person, one who does not rise to the occasion
Astrorisk:	star-shaped symbol identifying a heavenly body to indicate impending danger of colliding with another planet

Atall: ring of small coral islands in a lake located at a high altitude

Atomice: get rid of small dead rodents by disintegrating them

Attribrute: inherent trait of somebody who behaves like a beast

Auctionear: nearby public sale

Austear: so severe or strict that makes people cry

Avowel: open admission of something by just pronouncing the letter "a"

Aweigh: calculate the effects of something happening in a distant place

Awfool: not only horrible but stupid as well

Awegust: month of the year during which there are often strong, violent winds

Awkword: difficult word to understand or pronounce

Awryve: reach a place, but not as planned originally

B

“**B**e silent or let thy words be worth more than silence.” *Pythagoras*

Barister

Bacanal: orgy aboard a ship while navigating on a watercourse

Backlock: device to indicate hours and minutes which is slow

Bankquet: bankers' dinner to celebrate their bank' profits which jumped to record levels last year

Backwords: words read back to front, such as "ddo" = *odd*, "xo" = *ox*, "noom" = *moon*

Babee: a very young insect

Ballkanization: considerable reduction in some countries of the number of dance halls which nowadays can not stay open on their own

Bankhander: bank who issues preference shares without warning clients of the risks involved.

Barberity: cruel action committed by a hairdresser who shaves somebody with a faulty razor

Barister: lawyer who sells drinks in a pub in his spare time

Barock: of a large stone elaborately ornamented

Baronmeter: instrument for measuring the blood pressure of a member of the nobility

Basick: slightly ill

Baskit: container made of twigs in which a set of items for a specific purpose are kept together

Battory: group of influential conservative British MPs

Bazar: Russian oriental market in the times of Ivan the Terrible and later

Bayliff: person employed in a farm to prevent people from stealing the property of the landowner

Bay 6: cybernaut's term for "basics"

Beddable: obedient child who goes to sleep when told

Beefburglar: person who breaks into a butcher's to steal hamburgers

Beehave: make irritating buzzing sounds

Bee pee: derogatory term used by some petrol consumers to refer to the low quality of oil products when compared to those offered by other companies

Begpipers: street musicians who play a woodwind instrument in order to earn money from passers-by

Beknighted: related to a noble man who is an ignoramus

Belever: person who has been obliged with an iron bar to have religious faith

Bemewsed: puzzled by what sounds like a noise made by a cat which you cannot see

Beneaddiction: approval of a person's habit of acting or doing something

Benefishery: place where fish are caught that makes a profit

Benofficial: related to aid that has been legally authorized

Beshave: said of the proper conduct of a barber when using a razor in his job

Bewhere: warn about dangerous places

Bewhich: cast a spell over someone so that they can't decide "which" thing to choose

Biassed: said of someone with an innate predisposition to be a stupid person

Bibliofile: special folder in which a book collector stores their titles arranged in convenient order for reference

Biday: bathroom appliance for washing your private parts any time before midnight

Bike: short for Bichael, Michael's friend

Binister: person who becomes head of a government department for the second time

Biskit: set of ingredients for making small, flat cakes

Blasfamous: related to a well-known person who uses irreverent words about HOLY things

Blulster: loud and rough way of speaking which used to be common among some Northern Ireland people

Boardom

Boardom: dull, bleak territory "ruled" by male pigs near another country

Boath: solemn promise made by two people

Bonion: red welling on the big toe, probably due to eating too many onions

Boomeringue: small curved cake made of a mixture of sugar and egg white that always repeats on you

Booteeque: shop which sells woollen socks for babies

Bootique: shop that specializes in ladies' footwear

Boredon: dull, uninteresting teacher in one of the two British universities, Oxford or Cambridge

Boredroom: space within a building set aside for dull, boring meetings of the board of a company

Boath: solemn promise made by two people

Bonion: red welling on the big toe, probably due to eating too many onions

Boomeringue: small curved cake made of a mixture of sugar and egg white that always repeats on you

Booteeque: shop which sells woollen socks for babies

Bootique: shop that specializes in ladies' footwear

Boredon: dull, uninteresting teacher in one of the two British universities, Oxford or Cambridge

Bottocks: neurotoxin used for the treatment of wrinkles or any irregularities of a person's bottom

Boundairy:	line that indicates the limits of an establishment where milk products are made or sold
Boyant:	cheerful, lively young male person
Boysterous:	cheerful and noisy young male person
Bragmatic:	related to someone who boasts of being always a very practical person
Brandyshments:	flattering words uttered after drinking a considerable amount of alcohol
Braystorm:	disturbance caused by the repeated cries of a donkey
Breadatory:	referring to a person who steals all sorts of food made from flour, like bagels, baguettes, buns, biscuits, etc.
Breechess:	very comfortable trousers specially designed for chess players
Brickmanship:	risk of causing the collapse of a building by using construction materials of poor quality
Brigadear:	senior Army officer loved by those under his command
Buccanear! :	Loud shout given by the crew of a ship when a pirate boat is approaching them
Budgetaryan:	vegetarian who lives on a limited amount of money
Budjet:	aeroplane used by low cost airlines

Buccanear

Bulbus:	large, bulb-shaped motor vehicle for carrying passengers
Burzaar:	treasurer of an oriental market
Busybuddy:	friendly but meddlesome person
Byanyal:	happening twice every any two years

Bulbus

C

"Ce n'est pas la première fois que je remarque combien, en France particulièrement, les mots ont plus d'empire que les idées."

("It's not the first time I've noticed how much more power words have than ideas, particularly in France.")" George Sand, *Indiana*

Congergation

Cabort:	end the pregnancy as a result of excessive capering about
Cairopractor:	Egyptian medical person who treats injuries by manipulating muscles and the spinal column
Caledonion:	variety of vegetable with a bulb grown in Scotland
Calhorrific:	producing horrendously severe heat (or huge number of calories in some sweets and cakes)
Calibar:	diameter of the counter in a place where alcohol and refreshments are served
Calumnist:	journalist who publishes defamatory material
Camisoul:	spiritual element of a woman's garment
Campain:	excruciating activities organized in politics or business affairs
Canalyse:	study the possibilities of converting into a canal
Candidenture:	brilliant smile of someone hoping to be elected
Cannonaid:	extra bombardment to help recapture a position gained by the enemy / bombardment of assistance to a developing country
Cantanchorus:	of an ill-tempered group of singers who are unpleasant to deal with
Cantickle:	caressing chant used in church services

Capistation: special tax paid by taxi owners based at a bus or train station

Carcinomad: roaming epithelial cancerous tumour, not always malignant

Carefool: excessively prudent idiot

Carniporous: of an insect that feeds on the fluid that passes through the pores of humans and other fleshy animals

Cartilarge: larger than average elastic substance found instead of bones, especially around the joints

Cashmare: fabric made from female horse's hair

Categorecal: relating to a serious wound by the horns of an animal which causes the death of a person

Catharctic: related to the relieving of tensions and emotions produced by a short stay in the South Pole

Centiment: special feelings for money

Ceremoney: bankers' meeting to celebrate profits gained /formal occasion to raise money from participants

Circumlocations: outskirts surrounding an urban centre

Circonference: discussion that goes round in circles

Civiliced: relating to frozen water which is not unbearably cold

Clawsroom: room where learners are taught legal subjects

Coalesion: damage caused to one of the political parties who signed an agreement to work together

Coelision: temporary fusion of two or more political parties in which one of them has the upper hand

Coffeeine: same as caffeine, but more English vernacular-looking

Coinincident: unsuccessful attempt to insert 50 pence into a parking meter at the same time as a parking warden appears

Colicflower: vegetable that may produce severe pains in your stomach and bowels

Collesion: injury caused by running or crashing into something

Columny: fake architectural feature

Colonel sentence: basic, simple military expression such as "At ease", "Right turn", "Squad-halt"

Colossale: huge discounts on products

Combeernation: mixture of lager, bitter and stout

Comfordable: relating to the relaxing seating features of this car make

Commontary: ordinary oral or written description of something that is taking place

Compair: examine the differences between two individuals who are associated in some ways

Commeuppence: obligation to pay a small sum of money as a punishment for having done something wrong

Commonion: association of onion growers

Commonism: political theory based on people sharing the same characteristics

Compittance: ability to manage with little money

Complane: show dissatisfaction about the poor facilities offered by the airplanes of a certain airline

Complay: participate in a game with others in accordance with a established set of rules

Connact: take joint action

Concubanage: cohabitation in Havana and in the rest of the Pearl of the Antilles

Condoctor: medical person who directs an orchestra on weekends

Confax: confess one's sins by faxing them to the parish priest

Confermation: the act of confirming the decision to hold a discussion

Confez: admit responsibility for conspiring against the government in the third largest city of Morocco

Congaroo: variety of Australian marsupials known for their ability to dance salsa and other Cuban rhythms

Congergation: school of large marine eels who meet together to "pray"

Congesture: hypothesis based on a movement made with a part of the body, such as hands, head or eyes

Connhector: bully who boasts of linking people by introducing them to one another

Conqwest: the act of gaining territories on the other side of the Atlantic fighting against South American natives in the 16th century

Conseal: hide something under an official stamp so that it can only be seen by authorised people

Consieve: visualize an idea after separating it from others which are of a similar nature

Consirvative: related to a titled gentleman with right wing views

Consize: object of small dimensions

Consoledate: strengthen the feeling of compassion to make someone feel less sad

Consommation: the act of bringing to an end the eating of soup

Constractor: man who builds farm vehicles

Construth: result of something that you construe

Continew: resume doing something in an original and novel way

Convaless: not get better after an operation in the hospital

Coordonate: give away something acting jointly with other donors

Copiss: group of bushes and undergrowth at the side of a road where drivers often stop to relieve themselves or "water the flowers", if you like

Cornformist: person who doesn't object to eating any type of cereals for breakfast

Cornological: related to cereal crops stored in the order in which they are harvested

Corroad: destroy a track where vehicles travel by chemical action

Corrubberate: confirm a suspicion by finding that incriminating evidence had been erased with a rubber

Counseller: salesman who is also a member of a council

Countrybution: tax imposed by a rural municipality

Courteson: male descendant of a woman who exchanges sexual favours for money

Coweducation: training cows and bulls to improve farm productivity

Crazip: faulty device for fastening clothes; it might work properly or just as likely it might fail to work

Curtle: loose gown, shorter than normal, worn by women in the Middle Ages. (From Middle English *kirtle*; Latin *curtus*)

Customice: genetically modify pet rodents such as hamsters

Chaimbar: name given by the members of an institution to a space within the building where they can buy and consume alcoholic drinks

Chairful: related to a passenger who is happy to see that there are plenty of empty seats

Chairful: related to a passenger who is happy to see that there are plenty of empty seats

Chairful: related to a passenger who is happy to see that there are plenty of empty seats

Chairless: of a person who is sad because somebody else occupied the last empty seat

Chairy: careful when moving or carrying seats

Chamillion: person who changes his way of life when he wins the lottery in order to match his new social status

Champain: Sparkling French white wine whose expensive price leaves you with a feeling of discomfort if you cannot afford to buy it

Chancellar: person in a Government department in charge of the storage of wine

Characteristick: related to a clicking sound typical of someone or something

Charisman: male person endowed with such personal qualities and charm that cause people to admire and follow him

Chairitable: said of a generous person who gives seats to the needy

Cheesefake: cake that is not genuine

Chemistery: science which studies the substances that make up things and is difficult to explain to and understand by non-specialists

Chestairfield: extreeeemely large sofa only available on request

Chillblame: hold exposure to cold responsible for painful blisters on the ears

Chipmonk: member of a monastic order who is fond of squirrel- like animals

Choirten: hush a group of 10 singers in order to give them new instructions

Chronoilogical: related to events that are not arranged in the order in which they happened

Chucklet: type of food made from the seeds of cocoa which makes one laugh with satisfaction when eating it

D

“**D**o actions agree with words? There's your measure of reliability. Never confine yourself to the words.” Frank Herbert, *Chapterhouse: Dune*

Disguys

Dad cheque: money sent by parent to a student away from home, which is, unfortunately, less than expected

Dallyberation: discussion that lasts for more than the normal time

Daynty: pretty period of time when it is light

Dayism: old fashioned belief that God made the world in only one day

Deaconned: swindled by a lay assistant to the priest

Debutchery: over-indulgence in weekly meat consumption

Deadluck: hapless standstill

Deadpen: related to humorous writing which at first sight appears to be serious

Deafenit: relating to somebody who will never be able to hear again

Debillity: scarce number of charges to be paid

Decentery: acceptable degree of intestinal infection

Decibell: cup-shaped metal object that rings automatically when the level of noise surpasses certain limits

Decksterous: said of a person who is skilful walking on board a ship during bad weather

Declair: announce officially the location of a particular wild animal's den

Defar: postpone an arrangement to a very distant time

Defecake: wrong spelling, sorry!

Defiancé: strong resistance of a betrothed man to get married

Deflooration: the act of removing a tile floor to replace it

Defyne: challenge someone to provide a better definition of something

Delite: word form that some people belonging to the chosen few prefer to use rather than the standard word for expressing joy

Demice: end of mice entering a house by using expeditious methods

Demoat: reduce the importance of an impressive building to a much lower level

Demockracy: system of government where elected politicians make fun of the people who voted for them. In other words, government of the chosen people, by the chosen people for the chosen few people

Demonsterble: related to a frightening creature that can be shown to exist

Deodoorize: remove bad smells from the entrance to a building

Deplord: related to an a nobleman's instance of contemptible behaviour

Deputty: person acting as a substitute to fix glass in window frames with a soft paste

Deprivacy: the act of preventing someone from enjoying peace and quiet

Deskant: tune accompanying the main melody sung by a person sitting on a table

Deseast: give up holidaying in Eastern countries

Deseat: giving theatre goers seating with a poor view of the stage

Desend: new button on email programs to get embarrassing or inappropriate emails back

Despare: get impatient when you are free and you have too much free time

Detaiknee: middle joint of a leg in plaster preventing it from moving

Detestive: senior police officer that nobody likes

Detext: hate a certain piece of writing

Deturgent: very fast and efficient cleansing product

Devhour: read a three hundred page novel in 60 minutes

Devonair: related to a county in SW England where men are said to be courteous, polite and elegant

Devotea: a tea-drinking fanatic

Diabeetes: common disease in bees too

Diamateur: person whose hobby is distances across circles

Dielate: expand the time so as to pass away at a very old age

Dielect: minority language on the point of disappearing

Diffar: be very different, disagree completely

Dijest: take time to grasp a joke or witty remark made by another person

Dimention: measurement that is being talked about

Dinnersty: term used to refer to successive members of a family who attach great importance to enjoying the pleasures of the table

Disastral: severe damage caused by an object from space

Disavowel: disclaimer connected with the wrong pronunciation of any of the sounds represented by the letters "a", "e", "I", "o" and "u"

Disciplenary: rules of behaviour at meetings applied to all who are entitled to attend

Discoarse: rough, vulgar speech

Disrob

Disconsulate: relating to the overwhelming grief of a consul who has been given another posting

Diseas: unhealthy salt water not recommended for bathing in

Disenter!: Go out! Nonconformists are not allowed in!

Disguys: men wearing clothes so that people won't recognize them

Dispell: disregard the way in which the letters of a certain word are pronounced

Dispersians: Iranian refugees scattered in other countries because of social unrest in their region

Dispurse: spread out the small change on the table to count it

Disrob: take somebody's clothes off and then steal them

Dissemenate: distribute genetic material donated by men so that it can be properly stored

Dissemulate: conceal the fact that one is trying to do something as well as another person

Dissimolar: different back tooth

Dissuaid: convince somebody not to help others

Dissuede: persuade somebody not to buy a leather jacket

Distribrute: share out things in a rough, careless manner

Doormant

Disurn: distinguish among various vases that contain the ashes of a cremated body

Divorsee: person who, after a legal separation, has a clearer vision of his/her previous married status

Dominaunt: said of the sister-in-law of either one of one's parents who has a commanding influence on others

Domysticate: train some one to try and obtain union with God by spiritual contemplation

Doormant: related to a bouncer falling asleep on the job

Doormouse: small animal who has a special preference when trying to enter a place

Doubty: unsure person but brave and fearless when the occasion demands it

Downpoor: small fall of rain

Drinkmanship: the practice of consuming alcohol which can have disastrous consequences if carried too far

Dynamight: dynamite plus, a more powerful variety of explosive

Dynamow: cut grass with a lawnmower that also produces electricity

"**E**nglish words are like prisms. Empty, nothing inside, and still they make rainbows."_ Denis Johnson

Enormouse

Eatiology: study of the causes of being obese or overweight

Eeeee...: short for "elongated"

Easturner: person who goes back to live in his original country in the Middle or Far East

Echology: the study of the effects of reverberation on the environment

Echonomics: the science of producing cheap sound repetitions

Ecognomic: relating to the difficulty of understanding matters concerning the wealth of a country

Ecolocation: an ecological place, free from of any kind of pollution

Economess of scale: progressive deterioration of a country's wealth caused by inept political policies

Exstasy: intense feeling of happiness no longer present

Editoryal: article written by an editor who is a member of the British Conservative Party.

Edukation: training received by an earl in feudal times

Ed word: word containing the letters E+D, e.g., Edward, medal, redeem

Effrontiery: impertinent behaviour occurring on the boundary between two nations

Eggshibition: a display of a wide variety of eggs

Eggsorbitant: excessive price of the produce from chickens

Eggspertise: special skill in eggs matters

Egolitarian: of an immensely rich person who believes that all men are equal and entitled to the same rights and benefits as long as his/her privileges remain untouched

Ellips: perfectly formed oval-shaped mouth

Emandation: authorisation to correct errors

Emeragency: agency to help people who are going bankrupt

Emisery: person who is not happy as representative of his/her government in another country

Emonkcipate: free a monk from his religious vows

Emphartic: relating to flatulence released sonorously in a forceful way

Emplaicement: good location for catching flatfish

Empyrrical: relating to an experiment carried out at great cost

Emurge: appear very quickly

Enchoir: request information about a group of singers

Endoorse: sign the back of a cheque inside a building

Engauge: get involved in something after calculating its pros and cons

Enormouse: related to a larger than normal rodent with a long tail

Ensycholpedia: book containing extensive information about the study of the mind

Entree: access through a hole in a woody perennial plant

Enthrownment: ancient custom among some African tribes of throwing their future king into a as part of his coronation

Ephemoral: relating to decency and honesty lasting only a short time

Episoda: funny event involving the spillage of soda water

Equanenmity: controlled hatred

Equantity: the state of being equal in amount or number

Erhotic: related to a speaker of English who gets sexually excited when pronouncing or hearing somebody pronounce an "r" sound at the end of words like "sober"

Eroad: heavy lorries that wear away the surface of a road

Entree

Erucdite: person with an extensive academic knowledge who is often criticised because he has no qualms about belching in the presence of colleagues

Escapaid: the act of getting away from jail by bribing one of the guards for help

Esteam: regard highly the members of a group of workers

Esteamable: worthy of "esteam"

Evenduality: possibility of two events

Evernescent: related to something which disappears gradually

Evesdrop: what Adam's "wife" could never do

Ewesful: helpful female sheep that provides lots of milk to the family

Examiknee: injured knee being examined by a doctor

Examplify: demonstrate something by giving many examples of it

Exale: breathe out beer-smelling air

Excentric: no longer unconventional

Execushioner: official who puts a condemned person to death by smothering him

Exisle: island destination for people expelled from their native country for political reasons

Expertease: dexterity at provoking people in a friendly way

Expetition: journey of a group of people to make a demand of something

Excsell: be extraordinarily good at selling things

Excsell: surpass competitors in sales figures / outnumber sales made the previous season

Exsite: place which used to be of great importance but which, now, no longer arouses any interest

Exsize: taxes on large goods

Exqueezite: pressed together in a delicate, graceful way

Extint: colour which fades away and then disappears forever

Extramerital: relating to sexual relations outside the marriage which deserve praise for their discretion

Extremissed: related to a person holding radical views whose absence is regretted

F

“**F**or last year's words belong to last year's language
and next year's words await another voice.”
T.S. Eliot, *Four Quartets*

Feeline

Facsmile: reproduction of a happy expression

Fallowship: association of farmers who leave their land uncultivated to improve its quality

Famileer: relating to an all too common way in which some men look at young women

Famouse: Mickey is that

Fanfair: event where dealers exhibit and sell all sorts of cooling devices

Fanattic: person who is extremely enthusiastic about living in that part of a building just below the roof

Fantango: a mix of Spanish and Argentinean dances which will soon become fashionable

Fantaseized: person who can't escape from his fantasy world

Farawhy: distant, but for reasons that nobody knows

Far-cited: a famous phrase or words that will be quoted widely and profusely

Faritching: unpleasant irritation of the skin which continues to persist

Farmacy: shop on a farm which sells medicines for animals

Farmacist: person who sells medicines in a farmacy

Farsickle: ridiculous tool for cutting grass

Fartherland: distant country of origin referred to by nostalgic emigrants

Fartheast: the most eastern point of somewhere

Fartive: related to some one who releases flatulence stealthily

FAsia: dashboard made in a country in the Far East

Faulter: insecure, unstable person who makes mistakes

Faxemily: special fax format for women named Emily

Febrewery: beer factory that produces beer for one month

Feeback: return money paid in error

Feeline: queue of people waiting to pay money they owe

Feemale: alternative expression for a gigolo

F e g: wrong spelling of "effigy"

Fellowny: very serious crime committed by a comrade or by a member of an academic or professional association

Festiball: large formal social dance which takes place during the festival

Fewdal: related to a vendetta between a small number of people

Fewneral: ceremony held for a dead person which is attended only by a few members of the family and close friends

Filibastard: insult flung at somebody obstructing parliamentary proceedings by making long speeches to use up time

Filmsy: unconvincing, unsatisfactory motion picture

Fifteeth: replacing dentures five times

Finuncier: person or institution that lends money to convents

Flabbygasted: astonished at looking oneself in the mirror and noticing too much flesh hanging everywhere

Flatform: apartment near a train station

Flaygrant: related to a blatantly, shocking behaviour or situation which is severely criticized

Floot: stolen wind instrument

Flowary: relating to someone being chary due to flower allergy

Flulster: appl. to the verbal charm of people from Northern Ireland to confuse others with their arguments

Focus-pocus: deception after discovering that this Ford model has a production flaw in the engine

Forbedding: dark and dismal bedclothes

Forecite: ability to anticipate a quote that is going to be mentioned soon

Forecost: predicted price of something

Forfeet: donate one foot for a noble cause

Forthbright: brilliantly straightforward and honest

Fortwitters: digital illiterates who somehow manage to post tweets by sheer fluke

Fostar: promote an actor / actress

Franchase: try hard to get a licence to represent a company and sell its products

Freightful: risky, dangerous cargo

Frenattic: of somebody who behaves frantically in a top floor apartment

Frhenchman: loyal and trusty Parisian supporter

Frustrait: impede navigation on a narrow stretch of water

Fryten: fear of eating too much oily food

Fullish: unwisely filled to the brim

Funish: end something in a funny way

Funtastic: wonderfully amusing

Funzine: pleasant and amusing magazine which is enjoyed by lots of fans

Forfeet

Futourism:	tourism of the future.
Futourist:	person who will be travelling to different places for pleasure in the future

G

"**G**one. The saddest word in the language. In any language."
Mark Slouka, *God's Fool*

Gadjet

Gadjet: plane-shaped small device that can be used as a key ring

Gambet: plan to gain money gambling

Gangreen: environmentally-friendly group of young people

Gangstar: number one member of a group of violent criminals

Gaylic: happy-go-lucky way of speaking in Ireland and Scotland

Gayt: joyful manner of walking

Gaywalking: jaywalking in a happy and full of fun way

Gaurantour: organised trip that can be relied upon

Genethic: referring to the moral principles "most" human beings are born with

Geneulogy: speech to praise the history of a particular family

Genuinn: real, authentic small hotel

Genialogy: distinct cheerful and friendly generations of a family who all get on well together

Geranthology: collection of writings on aging and the health of old people

Geriattic: related to old people living in a small room in the roof of the house

Gerrymeander: proceed to divide a country for electoral purposes in a slow aimless way, as if reluctantly

Guestatory: related to the taste of entertaining a person at one's own house or table

Gigantique: enormous, old piece of furniture

Gimmnick: ingenious way devised by EU foreign ministers to spend public money on informal, relaxed meetings, whose outcome is not politically binding

Gineal: "congineal" alcoholic that makes you feel sociable

Glarmour: beautiful, protective clothing worn by celebrities

Glustre: shiny, splendorous town in the South West of England

Gobbledycook: jargon used by some cooks

Golpher: caddie in charge of keeping the holes clean from small rat-looking animals

Gonorrhreal?: gonorrhoea, for sure!

Goolag: muddy, sticky prison camp

Gosship: tittle-tattle about other people's private lives while on a cruise

Gothick: referring to the stiff consistency of some pointed arches of the architectural style of the 12th-16th centuries

Governuns: members of a religious female community whose job is to control and administer the business affairs of a convent

Graffeeti: markings or drawings on a wall made by a foot

Grammethics: new branch of linguistics whose aim is to promote the use of morally correct grammatical constructions

Grandmar: the mother of all grammars

Grannualation: the process of cropping up yearly grains of any cereal

Grammethics: new branch of linguistics whose aim is to promote the use of morally correct grammatical constructions

Grandmar: the mother of all grammars

Grannualation: the process of cropping up yearly grains of any cereal

Greatful: deeply, immensely appreciative

Gregorious: person who enjoys the company of people called Gregory

Greweling: increasingly difficult and tiring

GroSir: titled gentleman who sells food and other household items

Graffeeti

Grotask: related to a ludicrous, absurd job that needs doing

Grewsome: related to something gradually becoming horribly unpleasant

Grugbby: an even dirtier and muddier game than normal of this sport

Grumpee: ill-tempered and worried about the huge amount of liquid excreted by the kidneys

Guarantea: amount of tea offered as security for a loan

Guroom: Hindu spiritual leader who is getting married

Gurusome: repugnant Hindu spiritual leader

Gutteral: related to occasional harsh-sounding water running along a narrow channel round the roof of a house

Guyde: affectionate name used by tourists to address Guy, the person who shows them around

H

"**H**e wanted to cry quietly but not for himself: for the words, so beautiful and sad, like music." James Joyce, *A Portrait of the Artist as a Young Man*

Handicup

Hairess: woman who inherits a hairdresser's

Hairloom: lock of hair handed down to present descendants of a famous ancestor

Hairing: rare species of silver-coloured fish showing a distinctive filamentous outgrowth

Hallier: person who brings in the coal to large rooms

Handicup: small, damaged round container for drinking liquids that can be found on sale at a reject shop

Handsache: overenthusiastic greeting of too many people resulting in painful hand

Harbar: drinking establishment where ship's crews go as soon as they get ashore

Harlequeen: monarch wearing a fancy dress

Harmistice: temporary ceasefire which turned out to be not as beneficial as thought

Harmy: military organization which causes great damage to properties during training exercises

Harvast: plentiful crops

Havenuts: poor people who live on dry fruit

Hectair: unit of air equal to 10,000 cubic metres

Heedonism: paying attention to living a life of pleasure

Heedthen: non believer who, nevertheless, pays attention to religious customs

Hegemoney: economic leadership exercised by a country over others, as in Europe nowadays

Heirman: air force serviceman that has received an inheritance

Hellicopter: military aircraft specifically designed to strike fear into the enemy

Hellitosis: unbearably offensive-smelling breath

Helloh! : exclamation to show that you are shocked or surprised about what is happening, or what someone is doing.

Hemorrhaids: different drugs to counteract painful swellings inside the anus

Hereditor: person who "inherits" an editorship, usually a family member

Herpeas: disease causing red pea-shaped spots to appear on the skin

Hersuit: hairy woman's coat

Heterogenious: of a person who is extremely clever in many subjects and areas

Highdrophobia: very strong fear of water

Hi healer! :	common salute, when meeting a friend doctor, used by some people influenced by the Nazi ideology
Hoaks:	a lie, when told under the shade of an oak tree
Hoarsman:	man travelling by boat on horseback
Holicopter:	aircraft used by the highest ecclesiastical dignitaries
Holidaze:	period of time following a vacation when one feels confused or giddy
Holygarchy:	government by a few who believe themselves to be invested by a divine mandate
Homelette:	take away shop specializing in of food made from eggs
Homogenius:	said of a group of people with a similar degree of very high intelligence or special abilities
Hooligang:	band of vandals who behave wildly destroying things
Horroar:	fear caused by sounds like those of lions
Horrorscope:	prediction of horrible events based on the position of stars at the time of one's birth
Hospiss:	annexe to a house of shelter where pilgrims can alleviate themselves if in urgent need
Housekipper:	home-smoked fish
Hullocination:	imagining that someone is greeting you

Hoarsman

Hullograph: short handwritten greeting message

Hummingburgh: city in which hundreds of small birds make a continuous buzz

Humthinger: objects collector of remarkable excellence

Hurrycane: fierce storm approaching at great speed

Hypathetical: supposedly sad, but one cannot be sure about it

Hypnoties: put someone to sleep after first restraining the person

I

It is with words as with sunbeams,--the more they are condensed, the deeper they burn. *Robert Southey*

Iglue

Ibeerian:	Portuguese or Spanish person fond of drinking beer
Ichtheology:	study of the religion of fish
Icycle:	wheeled vehicle used by Eskimos
Idear:	a much cherished plan
Identistry:	distinguishing people by looking at their teeth
Idoll:	young child's favourite toy
Iglue:	modern Eskimo house made of blocks of wood (due to global warming) stuck together with a special adhesive
Ignawed:	of pets that destroy objects by biting them through lack of attention by their owners
Igsnore:	take no notice of the grunting noises made by your sleeping partner
Illeagle:	banned shooting of large birds of prey
Illisit:	related to resting on an unauthorised seat
Illustraitor:	artist who draws unpatriotic pictures of their country
Illuzionist:	person who makes people believe in a Palestinian Jewish community
Imachinery	futuristic device that only exists in an inventor's mind

Imbesilly: of somebody who is stupid and silly at the same time

Immaqueuelate: tidy, well organised line of people waiting for something

Immanure: dung not yet quite ready to be used as a fertilizer

Immencity: town of an extraordinary size

Imminant: relating to a small crawling insect about to appear

Immortar: new long-lasting cement used in construction

Impastor: a fake priest or religious leader

Impear: cause damage to pear trees

Impeckable: faultless, perfect kiss

Impertenant: insolent lodger

Implaw: beg the courts to administer justice

Imposeeble: non-existent and, therefore, invisible

Imum: mother of a Muslim imam

Inacsexible:: of a woman difficult to be seduced

Inadequote: inappropriate words by well-known politicians e.g. Bush's "weapons of mass production

Inadmissable: indispensable, absolutely necessary

Inadvisible: related to something that is unwise to look at

Inaffable: related to a very polite and friendly person that can hardly be described in words

Inbread: inborn predisposition to eat food made from flour

Inchoir: seek information about a group of singers

Incomesiderable: describing large sums of money received by top executives

Inconseevable: incapable of being seen

Inconsyllable: sadness of a word that has lost a syllable due to elision when pronounced orally, as in *secretary, arsenic, library, sedentary*

Incyst: doctors that keep trying to convince patients that a lump is not malignant

Indamnify: cursing someone you have to compensate for damage or injury

Indeafenit: related to someone deprived of the sense of hearing for a period of time not fixed

Indechorus: of a group of singers who show bad manners

indeuce: persuade a tennis player to reach quickly his opponent's score of 40

Indicater: person who points out others' needs

Indigenius: aboriginal of extremely high intelligence

Indiosyncrasy: characteristic way of behaving of the autochthonous inhabitants of the American continent

Indiot: foolish person from India who prefers to starve rather than eat a sacred animal

Indupitiable: sad, without any doubt

Inefestive: of some plan or activity not suitable for public gaiety

Ineight: of a person with inborn predisposition for numeracy skills

Infaction: the act of being contaminated by the ideas of a dissident group of people

Infantinside: criminal who murders a child indoors

Infiduality: situation in which both partners in a relationship are mutually unfaithful

Infur: deduce the probable social status of a person from the coat he/she is wearing

Ingrease: put on weight from eating too much fried food

Inkcident: unfortunate spilling of a coloured liquid from a fountain pen (over somebody's clothes)

Inkongaroos: unbecoming unusual features of some specimens of Australian marsupials

Inkwest: official investigation made in writing to find out the causes of something

Innascent: harmless, naïve person immediately after being born

Innattentive: relating to the poor service in a small hotel

Innbored: fed up with staying inside a small hotel

Insergeant: rebel officer who takes part in an uprising against the government of his country

Insite: provoke someone to do something *in situ*

Instractor: person who trains others to drive farm vehicles

Instrucked: lorry driver who has been ordered to drive to a particular place

Inteloper: person who meddles in a couple's decision to run away to get married

Intercause: action that produces an effect on several people

Interfear: to be afraid of participating in a situation which is none of your business

Interjet: interrupt someone with a remark when he is speaking about aeroplanes

Interknees: prisoners made to kneel on the floor of their cell

Interpurse: put coins in different handbags so that one always has small change available

Intrapid: fast-acting fearless person

Intrickate: deliberately complicated plan to deceive someone

Intrigger: person who devises a complicated plot involving the manipulation of an election to get a particular result

Introdeuce: announce that both players in a game of tennis have 40 points each

Invacation: prayer for a nice holiday

Invasian: influx of a large number of people from the Far East

Invenstory: detailed list of written fictitious events

Inverted comers: people who have arrived to live at a particular place and who show their homosexuality by signalling quotation marks with their fingers

Inzest: sexual intercourse between two members of the same family which they find very exciting

Irresalute: hesitant as to whether say hello or not

Irritaunt: exasperating sister of one's mother or father

Islender: money-lender living on an island

Isrealite: supporter of the old kingdom of Israel

J

"Just give me a thousand words and you may make your own pictures." Erica Goros

Jesture

Jargone: specialized, technical language which has fallen into disuse

Jazzmine: underground music bar known for discovering great jazz musicians fond of this climbing plant

Jesterday: a day of the week, not to be taking seriously

Jesture: facial expression or body movement made to amuse people

Jewbilant: of a Jewish person who feels very happy and satisfied

Jewbilee: one of the many Jewish celebrations held every year o

Jewellist: Jewish person who takes part in a fight between two people in order to settle a dispute

Judishushly: related to a sensible decision made by a judge warning the public not to make any comments

Jumboree: exceedingly large party and noisy merrymaking

Jumbow-sized: large weapon for shooting arrows

Justifireable: reasonable and rational dismissal of an employee

Juvenisle: referring to the Isle of Youth, second-largest Cuban island where Fidel Castro was imprisoned by the former dictator, Fulgencio Batista, after leading the failed July 1953 attack on the Moncada

K

"**K**ids use words in ways that release hidden meanings, revel the history buried in sounds. .....Words become incantatory. Open Sesame. Abracadabra. Perhaps a child will remember the word and will bring the walls tumbling down." John Edgar Wideman

Knight Club

KayOtic: related to a knockout which causes an uproar

Kg: cybernaut's short for "cagey"

Khartoonist: person from the capital of Sudan who makes humorous drawings in newspapers

Kingdame: politically correct expression for a county ruled by a female monarch

Kingpen: well-known editor of a prestigious newspaper

Kingsman: favourite male friend of a monarch

Kingswoman: wife of a monarch

Kneadle: long, rod-like wooden stick for mixing the various ingredients of a paste

Knightcap: alcoholic drink, usually pure malt whisky, taken by titled gentlemen before going to bed at night

Knight club: medieval pub where only brave soldiers to the king or feudal lord were admitted to drink and have fun late in the evening

Knightmare: distressing, unpleasant dream experienced by a titled "Sir"

L

"**L**ying is done with words, and also with silence." Adrienne Rich, *Women and Honor: Some Notes on Lying*

Licure

Laboreous: relating to a dull, difficult task

Lackernism: scarcity of varnish

La-dy-da: said of a pretentious woman who thinks she is superior to other people

Lafter: sound made five minutes after someone has told a funny joke

Lambment: faint bleat of resignation by a young sheep knowing what lies ahead!

Langauge: linguistic standard for measuring how well a person speaks or writes

Lanquid: weak state of sterling after falling 20% against the dollar

larinks: tube-shaped part of an ink bottle

Latintude: of a person who likes to cite phrases in the language of ancient Romans

Laufeeble: feeling weak after a fit of laughter

Laybar party: non professional group of people who get together in a pub for drinking and discussing politics

Leftenant: officer who is left-handed after having lost his right arm in combat

Leopardize: put a person at risk of being attacked by a leopard

lessbian: woman with a low degree of homosexuality

Leucosite: place where white blood cells can be located accurately, if necessary

Liarability: problems caused by skill at telling lies

Ligatour: trip around several geographical areas to connect people living there

Licure: alcoholic drink, usually taken after a meal, which aids recovering from illnesses

Lignight: type of coal of woody texture much darker than the ordinary one

Likelyhoot: probability that a siren may sound if one is not sure that it is disconnected/

Likelyhooked: of a fisherman unsure about whether or not he has caught a fish

Lingoist: linguist who can understand any style of language no matter how abstruse it may be . C.f. jingoist

Litteral: true, genuine rubbish

Loafar: perennial idle person

Lobotommy: surgery to enhance a person's buttocks

Locommotion: disturbance caused by moving excessively from place to place

Logarhythm: musical pattern produced by pronouncing a series of numbers

Londowner:	person who owns properties in London
Lonesum:	small, isolated payment
Lordable:	British nobleman who deserves being praised
Lordatory:	of a speech or piece of writing expressing praise for a Lord
Lowcation:	place for shooting films situated somewhere between +30º and -30º South latitude
Lowcust flight:	related to the plague-like spread of companies offering cheap air travel
Lullabye:	bidding farewell in a soothing way
Lunattic:	mentally unsound living on the top floor of a building

M

"**M**usic is only love looking for words."
Lawrence Durrell

to visit:
Paris
Madrid
Berlin
London
Next
Oxford
Liverpool
Edimburgh
Brussels
MAP

Motourist

Madamn: swear word used when dealing with an unreasonable and inflexible woman

Magistreet: legal official who judges cases in the open air

Magnifly: travel long distances by plane

Mainger: the largest container of food for cattle in a barn or stable

Mammouth: extremely obnoxious and boastful person

Manifeastation: ostentatious and high profile banquet

Manorism: characteristic behaviour typical of the owner of a large country house

Manotonous: related to a boring male person

Manover: manage to move something skilfully to a higher position

Mannekings: dummies to display the different military uniforms worn by monarchs

Marathin: extremely slim build of some long distance runners

Masterpeace: extremely successful agreement between two or more nations to stop an ongoing war

Masterpiss: first-class, remarkable pee

Maturnity: return to motherhood government policy in order to foster population growth (by rewarding women who produce more offspring)

Matrimoney: marriage arranged exclusively for chrematistic reasons

Mawning: canvas to protect a shop window from the sun during the first part of the day

Meanerpause: period in the life of a woman when she is bad-tempered due to hormonal changes

Meatery: butcher's shop

Meccanism: unconscious, automatic response by most Muslims to attend the prophet's call to visit Mecca

Medicaution: Being careful to take only drugs prescribed by your doctor

Medievil: great misfortunes which often took place during the Middle Ages

Mediocar: vehicle of average quality

Melancolic: very sad because of severe stomach pains

Memorabilious: referring to an irritable, unpleasant person who is only interested in collecting souvenirs

Mension: large building containing flats for men only

Merital: concerning the personal worth of marriage

Metehorologist: maker of weather clocks

Militourism: tourism involving visits to military bases and old battlefields

Minimale: small minded man who has become largely irrelevant

Monstruation: enormous monthly flow of blood expelled from a woman's womb

Moonsoon: period of full moonlit nights following the season of heavy rains in South Asia

Moresel: piece of food larger than normal

Motourist: person travelling by motorbike while on holiday

Mygrant: person who goes to another country to work and study with a scholarship from a university or other organization

Mytheology: the study of myths about religion and divine things

N

"**N**o one means all he says, and yet very few say all they mean, for words are slippery and thought is viscous". Henry Brooks Adams

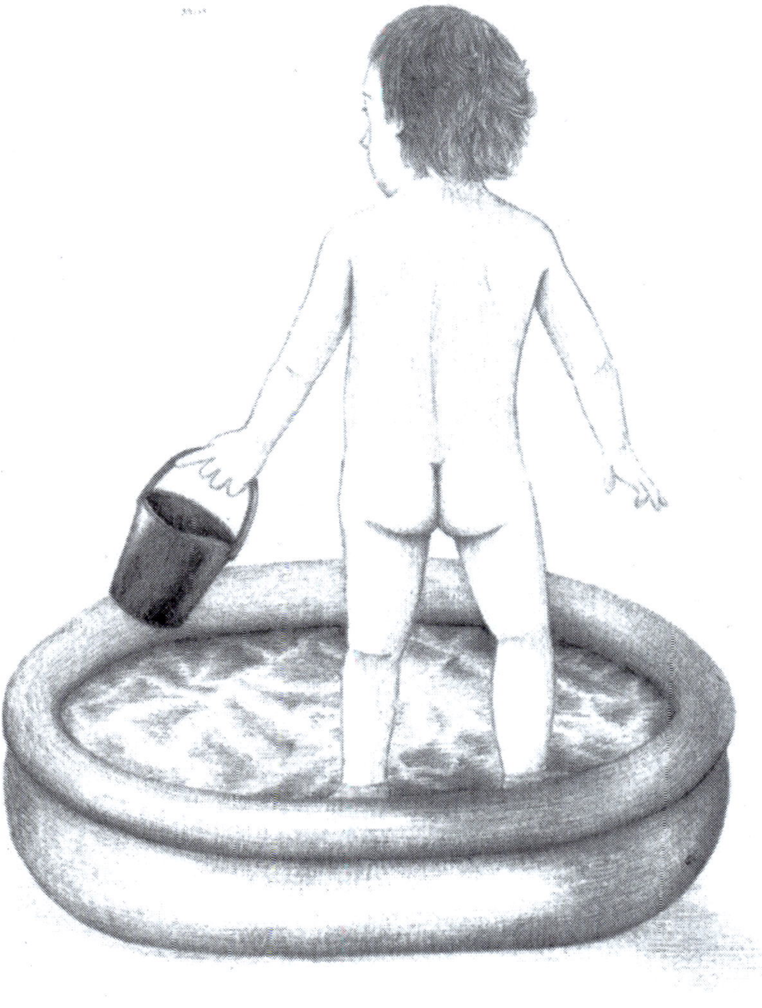

Nakid

NaEve: innocent female quality as if they were the first woman on earth

Nakid: related to a child who has no clothes on

Napsack: small inflatable rubber or leather bag used as a pillow when you want to sleep for a short time during daytime

Napking: short sleep often taken by a monarch during dull ceremonial occasions

Narrose: a not very wide passage decorated with flowers on either side

Neckst: invitation to a patient suffering from a contracture of the muscles of the neck to enter the doctor's office *"Neckst one, please"*

Neighbar: nearby establishment where alcoholic drinks are sold

Neighbarhood: area in a town where most of the bars are located

Neighbaring: pub crawling in the neighbarhood

Neighbore: uninteresting, dull person who lives near you

Newmonia: recently discovered disease affecting the lungs

Newralgia: twinge of pain appearing suddenly in any part of your arms or legs

Neurhologist: brain doctor whose hobby is to make watches

Newsrider: current affairs presenter who reports news riding a horse

Neutralies: invalidate the effect of something by telling things which are untrue, often used by political spin doctors

Newance: subtle difference in the quality of something which did not exist until now

Niceteas: free chocolates and biscuits offered by the best tea-rooms

Nighthood: covering for the head used by members of the nobility

Norseate: feeling sick when cruising around Norwegian fjords

Nunentity: female member of a religious order who feels herself to be of no importance

Nuntheless: despite being a female member of a religious community

O

"**O**ur words are giants when they do us an injury, and dwarfs when they do us a service." Wilkie Collins, *The Woman in White*

Oaseas

Oaseas: tiny island in the ocean with trees and fresh water

Obeisense: accept doing what one is told to do by inclining the heard forward

Objet: refuse to travel by plane

Obseen: of nasty, dirty things not to be watched

Observantory: place in a Civil Service department from which the boss can watch the work being done by his employees

Observerbal: of something distant that can be seen and accurately described orally

Obsexed: people with a high degree of prurience i.e. continually thinking about sexual matters

Obstackle: way of dealing with something which obstructs your way

Octover: tenth month of the year after which one can safely say that Christmas is round the corner

Oder: poet who suffers from halitosis

Oddyssey: long and rather strange journey

Ohgle: look at another person's nude body with lustful eyes, showing facial evidence of a pleasurable surprise

Olderman: an aged member of a borough or county council

Ombedsman: official appointed to investigate complaints regarding standards of sleeping equipment

Opportumissed: failing to take advantage of a lucky break

Orangbhutan: variety of large ape found in some regions of central Asia

Ordonation: voluntary pecuniary contribution made by someone who is conferred holy orders

Orfan: person devoted to helping children without parents

Origenial: of a fantastic new project or idea

Ornitheology: the study of winged divine creatures like angels, archangels, etc.

Orthoepee: (colloq.) the art of correct urination

Orthodocs: officially accepted documents

Orthodocks: officially approved port facilities

Ostemptatious: showing off how to resist being enticed by sinful thoughts and evil deeds

Osteoarthuritis: degenerative joint disease common among men named Arthur

Overdon: high ranking university professor teacher in Oxford and Cambridge universities

Overstop: go just beyond traffic lights that were red

Overum: having too much of a well-known, alcoholic Caribbean drink

P

"**P**eople to whom sin is just a matter of words, to them salvation is just words too." William Faulkner, *As I Lay Dying*

Pillionaire

Pacifeast: person who believes wars could be avoided if people devoted more time and energy to enjoying the pleasures of the table

Paedofile: information collected on suspects under investigation for this crime

Paraid: procession of police entering a building to arrest people who committed a crime

Paradogmatic: relating to an opinionated person who wants other people to follow his or her example blindly

Parentethical: related to something morally right said by a parent in the middle of a speech, but which is not essential to it

Partuition: sharing of classes between teachers

Passingers: people travelling by plane, train or ship carrying musical instruments and performing songs

Passivice: make a person take up an unhealthy habit by being exposed to it regularly, i.e. smoking

Pathfonder: person who loves discovering new routes across unknown areas

Patentea: person who has invented a new brand of tea

Patrimoney: inherited cash, bank accounts, pension, deposits, shares, etc.

Pawnchy: pot-bellied person used by others for their own benefits

Paygang: irreligious group of criminals who extort money

Pazoological: related to extreme love/hate of going to zoos

Peacemeal: food eaten pieceably, in a quiet, noise-free place

Pearings: circular, thin peelings from a pear

Pedegree: long list of university qualifications or awards gained by some students

Pedentry: the exaggerated manner in which some people enter a place

Peeple: group of persons urinating at the same time

Peknowledgeable: of a person who knows a lot about matters concerned with the punishment of criminals

Penalice: punish somebody by leaving them in a very cold room

Penhandler: person who stops you in the street to borrow your biro

Penisle: island with a rather phallic shape

Percushion: small, soft bag filled with foam rubber used by drummers and similar musicians to make their stools more comfortable

Perdiction: irreversible deterioration of the language as a result of poor usage

Perfodious: obnoxious, treacherous person

Periless: safe, not risky or dangerous

Peripathetic: related to a sad person who wanders aimlessly from place to place

Peritonightis: illness which often occurs late in the evening

Permissable: related to something that you are allowed to miss

Perplexcity: feeling of confusion caused by the size and noise of a large city

Perseveer: keep trying to do something but in a different way from the original

Persuaid: convince people to donate to good causes and charities

Pertenant: relating to something relevant to the person who rents a house from a landlord

Pestulant: said of a peevish and annoying person

Peternity: the never-ending status of being a father

Peternity leave: bylaw which, fortunately, has now been abolished

Phonethics: study of morally acceptable, nice sounding words

Phrance: European country whose politicians walk proudly in spite of unfavourable circumstances

Pieceably: done quietly, gradually, bit by bit

Pigsie: young, fairy swine

Pillionaire: very rich person who made a fortune by selling motorcycle seats

Pilow: light, thin travel cushion to rest your head on during a journey

Planely: clearly a type of aircraft

Plattitude: habitual manner to express truisms typical of some individuals

Playroll: list of actors to be paid in a theatrical company

Plottery: conspiracy involving a huge gamble of lottery tickets by a secret group of people

Plunch: fast food eaten at midday that is like a blow to the stomach

Poetester: writer of dull, uninteresting poems who assesses the quality of other people's poetry

Pollotion: the act of filling the air in an enclosed space with a smelly aftershave or ointment

Polygame: complicated arrangements of a man married to several women at the same time

Polygone: geometric figure used by a magician which disappears suddenly

Popaganda: the spreading of Pop Art and Pop music so that more people may enjoy them

Popagandist: an expert in the above

Porcupain: suffering caused by the quills of a rodent resembling a hedgehog

Porecity: shortage of openings/opportunities in a large metropolis

Pornbroker: person who acts as an intermediary in obscene transactions

Portugeese: white birds, larger than ducks, frequently seen in Portugal

Posterility: probable decrease in the future fertility of human generations due to the stresses of modern life and adverse environmental factors

Pozest: strong feeling that suddenly comes over you of pleasure at being alive

Precaries: unsafe condition of a tooth due to decay

Precreation: the condition of a woman who has started to consider getting pregnant

Presize: exact measurement

Predisease: illness which shows signs of imminent occurrence

Premonetary: related to a warning that something is going to happen to the currency of a country

Premonotion: feeling that an idea is about to pop into your head

Prepair: getting something ready for two people

Prisoon unoccupied public building destined to be used as a jail in the near future

Proaggression: increasing attacks on another country e.g. Russia against Ukraine

Prodigoal: said of a football player who scores many goals

Profassional: expert in fashion and styles of clothing

Projanitor: direct ancestor of a caretaker

Promblem: complication arising while on an unhurried walk or drive

Promissery: document guaranteeing meagre raise in salary

Promoat: raise a defensive ditch to a higher position for security reasons

Propence: of a British person who has the tendency to think in terms of his own national currency when he is abroad

Protext: show disapproval about the content of a written document

Provacation: the act of causing somebody to want to have holidays

Pshychologist: therapist specialized in treating people who suffer from timidity

Puerisle: said of a very young island, recently created as a result of a volcanic eruption

Punkctual: related to an unconventional youngster wearing outrageous clothes who never fails to meet you at the appointed time

Q

“**Q**uem diria que as palavras que nunca chegamos a dizer assentassem tão pesadamente?” _Jodi Picoult, *The Tenth Circle*

Quear

Qatarr: illness of the nose and throat, probably as a result of catching cold when last visiting Doha

Quache: tremble with pain

Quackmire: marshy area of land where only ducklings can walk across it safely

Quandairy: inability of a milk processing establishment to make decisions

Quantifire: calculate the amount of damages caused by a blaze

Quear: abnormal, strangely-shaped hearing organ

Queerantine: temporary isolation of strange people to prevent them making other nervous

Queery: odd, strange question

Quicksotic: fanciful, impractical but prompt to help and give with great generosity

Quoroom: space within a building where the minimum number of people required to pass a proposal hold a meeting

R

"**R**hythm. Life is full of it; words should have it, too. But you have to train your ear."Arthur Gordon, *A Touch of Wonder*

Repeter

R,r,r,r : bottom (see *a pain in the rrrr)*

Rabeed: related to an angry swarm of bees

Rabbye: affectionate closing in a letter or email for saying “See you soon” to a Jewish religious minister

Racontour: person who tells amusing stories about travelling in foreign countries

Ramadame: proposed Arabic title of respect of a woman to be used during the 9th month of the Muslim year

Rambanxious: energetic, boisterous person eager to obtain something

Ranchorus: embittered group of singers

Raydiate: emit narrow beams of light

Reashore: make sure that a boat has been safely docked and is not on the water

Rebillion: massive uprising against the government in which millions of people participate

Rebullion: popular uprising to obtain government's gold reserves

Recallcitrant: of a person who is reminded of being disobedient

Recipee: set of instructions to urinate properly

Rechoirement: licence required by a group of singers to be able to give their performance

Refactory: large dining hall converted into a building for the manufacture of goods

Refhuge: gigantic shelter to protect people in danger

Refhugees: massive displacement of people who are forced to go to a foreign country

Refoot: prove that what someone says is wrong because "the foot is on the other boot"

Refoundable: that can be rebuilt if necessary, without having to pay for it again

Regaylia: clothes, symbols and all kind of adornments worn by participants in Gay or LGBT Pride parades, dance parties and festivals..

Reggay: homosexuals' favourite Caribbean pop music

Regrain: harvest a second crop of cereals

Reguard: pay respect to a person wearing a military uniform

Regreat: be very affected by a bad decision

Reguelation: feeling of great joy and happiness about an official decision

Reimpurse: pay back a lady by putting the money directly into her handbag

Rejet: say "no, thank you" to an offer of travelling by plane

Rejoyce: to enjoy re-reading *Ulysses* and *Finnegan's Wake*

Rekingdle: stir up a movement in favour of the Monarchy

Relatavism: belief that very primitive feelings or behaviour is a changing truth, depending on circumstances

Relavatory: describing the experience of using one of those very hi-tech toilets

Releave: feel alleviated after abandoning a dull place

Relegion: legionaries' creed

Relinquiz: give up answering trivia questions

Relucktance: unwillingness to accept that something good has happened to you

Remoat: defence round a castle located very far away

Renoun: a word which became famous for unknown reasons

Repeter: parrot who pronounces Peter over and over again

Reprihand: punish a young child by spanking them

Resergeant: non-commissioned officer who reenlists in the Armed Forces

Resqueue:	offering to keep someone's place in a line when they go to the toilet
Retyre:	get rid of the worn parts of the wheels of your vehicle
Revalley:	wake-up call when they are camping in a low area between mountains
Rhinotis:	inflammation of the nasal mucous membrane of a rhinoceros
Ridicallous:	insensitive to people's problems by making making stupid remarks
Roedema:	homemade treatment to redeem discomfort caused by fluid retention
Roomatic:	feeling pain and stiffness in the joints of muscles due to spending long hours sitting in a damp place in the house
Rotundra:	vast, circular, flat area in the Arctic regions where the ground is permanently frozen
Rowman:	citizen of Rome who sculls on the river Tiber
Rumbastious:	relating to a noisy, cheerful person who is fond of Cuban music
Rumpage:	wild behaviour after getting drunk with liquor made from the juice of the sugar cane

S

"**S**weet words are like honey, a little may refresh, but too much gluts the stomach." Anne Bradstreet

Sunctuary

Sabbattical: period of time during which a university teacher is exempted from teaching to carry out research in an attic

Sacriface: saving someone from embarrassment by accepting the blame for something

Sadderday: gloomy weekend day, worse than expected

Sagracious: pleasant, courteous person who has an acute sense of judgement

Salava: hot feeling in the mouth after eating a very spicy curry

Salaxcity: careless, incorrect way of showing or dealing with sexual matters

Sarcaustic: related to very unpleasant, cruel remarks

Satelight: very small bright object moving around the earth

Satirety: the state of being fed up with ironic, negative criticisms

Scarecity: place where there is an acute shortage of consumer goods and facilities e.g. Caracas, in Venezuela

Scavengeance: desperately looking for even a little revenge

Schistematic: habitual participation of someone in activities of religious sedition

Scianthology: collection of writings dealing with a religious movement founded in the USA in the 1960s

Scrhomage: tribute paid to rugby players

Scupidity: foolish greed for money or possessions

Semenar: small class for discussions and research into matters related to genetic material

Sementics: another term for semenology, the study of the meaning and quality of human semen

Senascent: related to an old person who is born again (figuratively) after escaping a serious body operation

Senisle: geologically old island

Shache: pain caused by trembling

Shallfish: fingerling, sea animal in the making that has a shell

Shampooh: poor quality liquid for washing hair

Shenanigangs: bankers who use all kinds of tricks with their clients

Shoury: related to the weather when it rains heavily for 60

Shoredid: dirty, unclean seaside

Showvinism: eagerness to demonstrate the love for one's country/ clear demonstration of sexist attitudes

Shystar: dishonest celebrity

Signnusitis: blocked nose and headache indicating that the sinuses of a person are swollen

Sinistar: forbidding celestial body

Sinseer: earnest, honest prophet

Sircumspect: related to the discretion and cautiousness of a gentleman

Sirencester: market town in Gloucestershire, England, famous in Pre-Roman times for the excellent breed of bovine male parents

Sirendipity: discovery by chance of a very beautiful woman

Sirmon: religious speech delivered by a lay man

Sirtify: confirmation by a respectable gentleman of the validity of something

Slaugh: lose cheerfulness and be sad

Smere: a very small smear

Snighper: person who fires shots from a short distance away

Sojournalist: person who writes for a newspaper and lives away from home for a time

Somenolent: just a bit sleepy

Soupervise: oversee the cooking of soup to make sure that it is done properly

Sorarity: peculiar, uncommon club of women students at some American universities

Souvenear: object that one buys as a memento of a nearby place recently visited

Spectocular: impressive, breathtaking when seen through a telescope

Spooradic: of a mark left here and there by an animal

Springbored: of a swimmer who is fed up with jumping into the water

Spyneless: lacking the necessary aptitude and qualities to be a spy

Squeagle: curved line made in the air by a flying large bird

Squeel: shrill scream given by an eel when some one steps on it

Sqworming: the way a worm moves around

Stewpendous: exquisite, delicious cooked dish of meat

Strickt: disciplined, cunning action to deceive someone

Sucsession: meeting, event which follows next in order

Suffergettes: women who still experience hardship fighting for equality

Sunctuary: pagan holy place to worship the Greek god Helios

Supervice: monitor the criminality index in a country

T

"To care about words, to have a stake in what is written, to believe in the power of books - this overwhelms the rest, and beside it one's life becomes very small."

Paul Auster, *The New York Trilogy*

Toylet

Tailord: relating to clothes specifically made for a member of the nobility, such as a duke or a marquis

Taxenemy: method of classifying people who hate having to pay taxes

Taxiturn: quiet taxi driver who speaks very little

Teatotaller: person who doesn't drink tea at all

Teenacious: of a person in his/her teens who is persevering and resolute

Telegrammar: mobile phone application for teaching the grammar of a language

Televice: broadcast on television news related to pornography, drug trafficking, etc.

Testimoney: bribe offered to a witness to influence his or her declaration before a judge

Therapee: psychological treatment for urinary incontinence

Therapissed: 1) trained professional whom a child peed all over during urinary incontinence treatment; 2) drunk therapist

Therapewtic: relating to the treating and cleaning of high backed benches in a church

Therminology: terms and expressions used in matters related to heat and temperature

Thoroughfair: road leading directly to an exhibition of farm produce or livestock

Togatherness: intense feeling of pleasure at having assembled things which were scattered all over

Toylet: plaything for very young children who are learning to use the bathroom

Transfar: senc something from a place to another very distant one

Tripartight: government by a closely linked coalition of three parties

Trugstore: shop which sells garden baskets for carrying flowers, etc.

Tunique: sole, exclusive woman's outer garment reaching to the knees

U

“**U**sing words to talk of words is like using a pencil to draw a picture of itself, on itself. Impossible. Confusing. Frustrating ... but there are other ways to understanding.” Patrick Rothfuss, *The Name of the Wind*

Urbin

Unawhere: not to know where one really is

Umbiblical cord: link joining some very pious people to God and through which they receive spiritual nourishment

Underdon: in the universities of Cambridge and Oxford, a teacher below the rank of a don, a sort of assistant

Unpolooted: uncontaminated area of a city which has a low burglary rate

Unpresidented: of a person who has never been a president before

Unreworded: of a writer still waiting for payment for a recently published novel/unsuccessful new written text after being stylistically revised

Updeight: upgrade to Windows 8 versions

Upendicitis: vertical position of a person's appendix

Urbanight: person who lives in a city and enjoys wondering about at night

Urbin: large city container for waste materials

Urnings: money made by selling urns

Uxorcize: free one's wife from an evil spirit or harmful influences by praying

V

"**V**ocabularies are crossing circles and loops. We are defined by the lines we choose to cross or to be confined by." A.S. Byatt

Valewe

Vacansea: job opening on board a ship

Valewe: valuable female sheep

Variasians: different kinds of people living in the Asian Continent

Veinglorious: said of a person who is very proud of his/her perfect venous system

Ventoxity: flatulence produced by the possible ingest of poisonous food

Veteurinarian: specialist in animals' urology

Viewsually: see something frequently

Vineglory: pride in one's wine cellar

Visability: ability to visualize

Visistation: visit paid at a train or bus station

Vissit: go to a particular place in order to rest one's buttocks

Vituoperative: effective way of using harsh, insulting language

Vivicious: lively, but sometimes violent person

Volgarity: uncivilized, tasteless behaviour taking place on the river Volga

W

Words are things; and a small drop of ink, falling like dew upon a thought, produces that which makes thousands, perhaps millions think.

George Gordon Byron

Wedther vane

Walloh: express delight at a life being lived with luxury

Warfair: an exhibition of military technology

Wayl: make long, high-pitched sounds while walking or driving along a street

Weakday: any day when you are not feeling 100%

Wearisum: a large number of items which is tiring to count

Wedluck: a fortunate marriage

Wedther vane: instrument on the roof of a building which points out the direction to the place where a wedding is being celebrated

Weekling: person without the strength to get up on a Monday

Weepee: related to a child who cries because he peed his pants

Weighlay: stop people in the street to ask how heavy they are

Weighter: person in a thrifty restaurant whose job is to measure the amount of food served to the table

Whatshit: vulgar manner of referring to the name of something that we have forgotten

Whensday: a day in the week when you suddenly realized that you have forgotten an important date e.g. Your wife's birthday!

Whoremones: chemical substances found in the body that make you want to have wild sex

Whyly: clever person who gets what they wants by asking tricky questions

Wreckognize: acknowledge that something has been totally destroyed

Wreckompense: give somebody compensation for irreparable damages caused to their property

X

Xorry! No quotes beginning with this letter

X-lover

X-lover: former partner in a romantic relationship

X-husband: former husband

X-wife: former wife

Y

"**Y**ou couldn't leave words lying around where our enemies might find them." Margaret Atwood, *The Year of the Flood*

Youngstar

Youngstar: child who became famous as an artist

Youthanasia: the act of helping young people to die who are suffering from an incurable illness

Z

"**Z**eal without knowledge is like expedition to a man in the dark."
Isaac Newton

Zerow

Zealottery: excessively eager desire to win money by gambling

Zerow: seats in a theatre just below the stage

Zupper: person who keeps changing TV channels while eating their evening meal

Flying birds have no master

(French proverb)

My puns

1. I took her hand only for the shake of it.

2. For little Johnny's 4th birthday his parents bought him a toylet

3. As a matter of flat, he lives on the 2nd floor

4. Get back to Bay 6 and your quality of life will improve

5. As there was no visible axes, I couldn't get into the house

6. After the two Mafia families agreed that shared possession of the island was the best compromise they could reach, they stopped fighting each other and signed an agreement for a long-lasting piece.

7. Everybody knew he was French because of his peculiar arse

8. When the Court refused to recognize his title the heir was blue

9. Inexplicably, all members of the Board jumped with joy when they were summoned to meet in the Chain bar.

10. As his doctor recommended cold Turkey to quit smoking, Jim bought warm clothes to wear during his stay in that country

11. Parents with good quality jeans normally pass them on to their children

12. There was no moon when the knight fell down during the battle.

13. In my haste to answer your e-mail, I Mr Why; (I wrote "the" instead of "they")

14. If you're P.Ann, you are supposed to know the name of the current President of France

15. His decision to desecrate the picture of St Nicholas was holy unjustified.

16. Due to budgetary restrictions, the Department of Botanics could only book a locust flight to combat the plague in situ.

Typeset and printed by
Ahoradigital
Pintor Ribera, 15
38007 S/C de Tenerife
Tel.: +34 922 20 03 52
E-mail:imprime@ahoradigital.es

8371471R00116

Printed in Great Britain
by Amazon.co.uk, Ltd.,
Marston Gate.